In Case You Didn't Hear Me The First Time

Poetry and Prose by Sharon Skinner
ISBN: 978-1-938190-22-3
©2010 Sharon Skinner Enterprises
All poetry and prose written by Sharon Skinner

Design & Layout by Bob Nelson, Brick Cave Media

Cover Photograph VLA, New Mexico
Cover Photograph ©2005, 2010 Sharon Skinner
Back Cover Photograph Courtesy Siren Studios

Illustrations ©1995, 1997, 2002, 2009, 2010 Sharon Skinner

Photographs ©1979, 1997, 2010 Sharon Skinner

Contacting Sharon:
Sharon Skinner
PO box 4411
Mesa, AZ 85211-4411
www.sharonskinner.com

Brick Cave Books
2010
Mesa, AZ
www.brickcavebooks.com

To my husband, Bob.
I love you more.

Table of Contents

1	—	SEATTLE 2001
3	—	DANCE ON
4	—	HEADLINE: ARTIST PAYS TAX DEBTS WITH SKETCHES
6	—	MY BLOOD
7	—	ISOLATION
8	—	SUMMER COMES
9	—	SUMMER'S END
10	—	VACUUM
11	—	FIVE QUESTIONS
13	—	DIEGO GARCIA
15	—	SUNFISH
16	—	SHORT-TIMER
20	—	D.C.
22	—	GUNS
23	—	YOU
24	—	INHALING
25	—	PEOPLE WATCHING
26	—	THE GOLDEN GARDEN
27	—	AGAINST MYSELF
29	—	SOMETHING MORE
30	—	DEADLINE
31	—	IN THE FIRE
32	—	UNDRAWN SHADE
33	—	FINAL RELEASE
35	—	ON A GOOD DAY
36	—	YOUR PASSING
37	—	ANOTHER GRANDMOTHER POEM
38	—	MY MOTHER CYBER-DATES
40	—	COTTON CANDY
41	—	ADA'S WISH
47	—	REGRETS
48	—	MEMORY
49	—	THE CUPBOARDS MATCH THE FLOOR
50	—	NIGHT BIRDS

51	—	VEILED MOON
53	—	SHADOWCASTER
56	—	EBB AND FLOW
57	—	MOONFLOWERS
58	—	STATUESQUE
59	—	PERCHANCE . . .
60	—	FLOATING LEAVES
62	—	TIME CURVES
63	—	COLD NIGHT
64	—	LOST ART
65	—	THE DANCER
67	—	THE VULTURES ARE CIRCLING . . .

SEATTLE 2001

Amidst the rainbow flag waving and
black-power fist raising,
in the language of La Raza,
"Yo tengo una causa."

And I have something to say.

I used to think I had to be mute,
that I,
a mere white woman,
had nothing to say.

But I have lived many lives,
I have been reborn,
and I know this:

I know that a four-year-old child knows the difference between "good touch" and "bad touch" without ever being told.

I know that all people are capable of good, as well as bad—
that the color of your skin does not make you better or worse,
      and that color is politics and politics is color.

I know that Yin and Yang are eternally and inextricably entwined.

I know that my ancestors went to war naked—
wearing only blue paint and the heads of their enemies tied at their waists—

      and I am filled with the blood of my ancestors!

I know that people will make excuses for hate and never let go of the past.

I know that violence sells,
                hate is interesting,

and a southern accent doesn't necessarily prove ignorance.

I know that the left wing is continually opposed to the right wing—
>but it still takes two wings to fly.

I know that the fears after ten years clean aren't any different than the fears after being clean for ten days, except that . . .

>I know that I can get through another "one day at a time" and . . .

>"look ma, no tracks."

DANCE ON

Dance on my friend.
The fire of life is beyond us now,
the edge of the world begun.
The meaning inside ourselves is set,
a place where the old is besieged.
The natural bridge of our body unkept
is awash in the rising flood,
As the rain pours down like the sweat of the flowers
in heated young fields where we lie.
Yes, dance on my friend
to the harp of the moon
and the lyre that sings from the stars.
The tune we all hear is the sound of our hearts
in the struggle of safety and fear.

Headline:
Artist pays tax debts with sketches

My aspirations come with inspiration and resonate
  like the exhalations of the dying,
   while "Notebooks of Shit" are used to pay tax debts in foreign countries.

My life's work has mainly been to stay alive
  despite dangerous behavior and covert suicidal tendencies.
I deliver now on the promise of what can be,
  on potential and possibilities.

And now, even when the sky falls, I get back up, (not without a little help).

I am learning to fail successfully, to take an easier path.

I look out at time and time lost,
  and begin to see the similarities between them
  and the open space where rest and dreams are not
  mortal sins.

I am recovering and uncovering and
  beginning to understand just how much I do not know,
  will never know, and never miss.

I have been half way 'round the world and
  as far away as I can travel my critics are always near,
  living within me and ensuring my guilt.

I have remade myself more times than Madonna,
  sometimes out of longing, often out of fear,
  and once out of desperation.

In an undiscovered country, I am a newfound secret.

The wisdom of my mother is revealed in the knowledge that
  I am divergent.

The love of my husband is a garment that is always clean and beautiful,
  but sometimes more than I can bear to wear.

It is in the darkness of my soul that I still dance.
It is in the desperate motivation of my spirit that I still soar.
And it is in the hollow places of my personal night that
  I still find the power of creation.

I am not an artist who creates form beauty and light,
I am a poet who screams from the depths.
My inner energies burn with the heat of a thousand suns,
  and yet I lie comatose in the ruins of my own innocence.

I climb an unending staircase, winding, spiraling,
  searching for the end of the maze and safe haven.

  The urges never die, I just try not to look down anymore.

And when I find myself in meadows of gold
  and valleys filled with sunlight,

I inhale the freedom of the dream and count my blessings.

my blood

My ancestors were pagans
Gaelic warriors who faced battle
Naked but for the blue woad
staining their skin

They prayed to animal gods
To the sun and the moon
Trees and the great mother
Earth

The triple goddess walked among them
Priests and druids taught
the secrets of life
And sacrifice

Sword and dagger
Plaid and steel
Clan and tribe

My ancestors valued honor
Bravery, courage and loyalty
They paid their debts with sweat,
Blood and gold
Swore fealty and were steadfast

Gifted and dauntless

They have given me a legacy

The need to be more

A desire that lives in my heart
And is seldom quiet

ISOLATION

The soul, alone, encompasses the grid of spiritual being.
Affront the self and be unmade in all the conscious world.
I gave myself into myself, a hole of blackest night,
And cheered myself with ringing song, to keep the demons clear.
But in my selfish solitude I did not realize
The coldest, darkest, cruelest plague was written in my eyes.
As fear bred fear and fear contempt of what I did not know,
The monster that I feared the most was never very far.
And when the shields were all in place, protection seemed assured.
Until I found that, I myself, was who I feared to meet.

SUMMER COMES

Sneaking, sweltering.
Sweat-moist bodies in
dry, crackling air.
Absorbent sand.
Heat radiant rocks.
Thorn rippled cacti.
Small shaded sanctuaries
where bird and reptile
vie for position,
predatory instinct
and wild animosity
saved for cooler times.
Bare bleached acres undulate,
shimmering in rising waves.
El Sol, soul of the desert,
glares without remorse.
Withered stalks of ungreen
whisper, sh-sh-sh-sh-sh-h-h-h,
stay out of the sun.

SUMMER'S END

The year smiles drily.
Desert sun setting slowly,
clinging to the horizon,
waiting as patiently as a soaring vulture
for the last day of summer to die.

Fall comes slowly,
an illusive dream that shifts and shimmers
in the mist of heat that rises from desiccated
sand and burning rocks.

Winter is a distant echo
mocking us as snowbirds flock,
seeking space in a soon to be oasis
of neutral temperatures,
dry air,
and mild nights.

Phoenix,
bright bird of legend,
fades to ash,
waiting to be born again
in late spring.

Our sphere spins on,
redundantly,
but what of tilt and wobble?

We can only pray.

VACUUM

It isn't true, what they say about space.
It's a matter of distance and time.
Where a wrinkle or curve makes a difference of light and
the bending is seen from the past
as a shimmering glow in the sky of our future
where our nursery rhymes are sung.
And the rocking we feel
is a shift in the field
of waves that we swim within.
The pull of the mass at the edge of our thoughts
is gravely in tune with our hearts,
where the sky has no limit or final frontier, but
the path of the orbiting dust.

FIVE QUESTIONS

Posted on 2007.03.05 at 16:50
I've been memed by pedantka

Here are the five questions she posed with their respective answers.

1) I know you're a pretty damn good writer, and I think you just mentioned that you paint. Any other creative outlets?

(Here is where my ADD really shines.)

Actually, most of my abstracts are done in pencil, but I have dabbled in paint. I also have done a number of chalk and charcoal still lifes. In fact, I am a major creative dabbler, and have tried my hand at an array of things, including sculpting (clay), some woodwork, and various combinations of mixed media.

Some of my best work is with fabric and fibers. I have the ability to translate just about any picture into embroidery, I sew costumes without patterns, and I have done some pretty amazing fabric sculptures. As for needlecrafts, etc., I have done several types of weaving, and have also quilted, knitted, crocheted, and tatted. Although, I didn't tat much or for long. As with a number of things, I just wanted to learn how it was done.

I did theater for many years, and was a drama major when I first entered college (an eon ago). I did the usual tap, jazz and ballet as a kid, and later got involved in ethnic dancing, and then taught belly dancing for eight years.

I played clarinet in school and guitar for a number of years, and have recently been toying with a tin whistle. My heart is set on one day playing the Celtic harp. I've sung with a number of groups, including the Sweet Adelines.

I also like to cook, but rarely use recipes except for very complicated new dishes, or as a reference to see if what I want to do has ever been done before.

2) Guilty pleasure?

Television (I am particularly fond of detective and forensic science programs because I used to install and repair medical & laboratory equipment) & Urban Fantasy Novels.

3) What's the weirdest job/work experience you've ever had?

At my age, there have been so many! Working in the hospitals and laboratories offered many an opportunity to see wild and unusual things. Watching the entire Arabian horse studding process was pretty weird. However, if I have to pick one, I'd say that seeing the collection of items one hospital had removed from certain human orifices pretty much takes the weird work experience award.

4) I'm passing this one on to you: what is your personal golden rule, and why?

Be kind. I generally am of the opinion that tact is for weenies. However, I am putting forth a concerted effort to be a kinder, gentler person. Although, I think I may adopt your golden rule of Sh*t Happens. It covers the kindness angle pretty well, while also allowing for f-ups.

5) You've just won the Booker Prize. How do you celebrate?

1) Jump up and down, bounce around the room, do a general happy dance and scream out loud. (Yes, I would really behave that way.) 2) Post it to my blog, call my family, and email everyone I know. 3) Book my dream vacation to the British Isles where I will do research for my next book.

DIEGO GARCIA

      The small island of Diego Garcia, located in the Indian Ocean, looks like the outline of a human footprint. It has even been called the "Footprint of Freedom." From tip to tip, the island is a mere 37 miles long, and no more than one quarter of a mile across at its widest point. It is a thin strip of land that curves in a long narrow U-shape to become the outline of the foot, forming a natural harbor that is thirteen miles long and six miles wide. Three tiny islands, bird sanctuaries actually, lie where the three middle toes of the foot would be. Ships exiting the harbor area sail between the toes before heading for the open sea.

      It may be different now—I hear the Navy has built a large cement pier that invades the harbor where vessels can tie up rather than anchoring out—but when my ship was there in '80-'81, the island was nearly pristine. The water was so clear that we stood on the boat decks watching schools of bright yellow sunfish swim in and around the shadow of the ship. They would ebb and surge, swimming in a quiet deceptive calm, which was broken only when a long black barracuda shot out like an arrow from under the ship and struck one of the colorful creatures, carrying it off for an afternoon snack.

      From the short wooden dock where the small boats and liberty launches tied up, you could look down on iridescent tropical fish and flowing-finned lionfish, as if seeing through clear glass into a well-lit aquarium.

      The U.S. leases the island of Diego Garcia from the British, a long-abandoned copra colony with the ruins of ancient coconut plantations still visible. The only animals on the island—besides the coconut crabs, known for their powerful grip—were a few mules, cats, and chickens, descended from the domestic animals left behind when copra was no longer of any great value and the plantations were abandoned.

      A number of British representatives were stationed on the island, sent there to ensure that we (the "Ugly Americans") did not damage the "queen's property." Fines were handed down to any sailors who were ignorant enough to disrespect and disturb the graves of those who were buried in plantation soil or otherwise harass the native flora or fauna. It was considered a joke that a fine could be levied for touching the Queen's asses, cocks, pussies, or crabs, but it could be frightfully expensive if one did not take the warning seriously.

When the crabs migrated across the island, the ground was covered with them. One could not drive two feet without hearing the crrrunch, cr-rrunch, crrrunch of the crabs' demise. Or the much quicker crunch-crunch-crunch-crunch when a gang of bored sailors decided to drive faster and aim a little better.

For some reason, when crabs migrate they don't care what is in the way. Rather than go around, whenever possible they walk right over whatever obstacle lies in their path in a focused and determined manner. Not that they had to make a long trip to cross Diego Garcia. There is a spot on the island where, by stretching a bit, a person could straddle the narrowest part of the island and stand with one foot in the bay and the other foot in the Indian Ocean.

The island is covered with huge coconut trees, and we quickly learned to judge the ripeness of the fruit and how to invade the outer shell to get to the sweet milk and meat inside. We were warned about sea snakes and poisonous coral as well, but I never saw any of those deadly creatures. What I did see was the beauty of a tropical paradise that knew no romance—fraternization being against Naval regulations and almost as costly as disturbing the queen's animals—only the comings and goings of our naval forces, activity that reminded me of the migrating crabs. Along with a film of engine oil, diesel, and the detritus of civilization, the marching feet of military personnel, left behind on this tiny atoll, their footprints, dissolving in the surf-washed sand.

Sunfish

Yellow suns
floating
in a liquid sky.

Orbiting,
they drift and sway,
in hypnotic universe.

Barracuda,
black comet of
death.

Sad solar burnout,
ultimate winter for
one lone sun.

Shattered crystal water
refracting into
glittering
darkness.

Until . . .
Hypnotic universe
appears once more.

Endless ocean
filled with
yellow suns
floating
in a liquid sky.

Short-Timer

I have heard people say that each time one door closes a new one opens, that endings are only beginnings seen from the other side. The truth of this became clear for me many years ago on the day I was discharged from military service with the United States Navy.

It was a bright day in Hawaii, the sky a perfect powder blue. Small white clouds drifted overhead, and the water sparkled like a shattered diamond, light bouncing off wave crests in a glittering, luminescent show of rainbow colors.

I had been counting down the days in military tradition, using a "short-timer's calendar." Every day had a number, and with each day that was crossed off the numbers grew smaller. I'd started my calendar a full year prior to my discharge date, and had religiously X-ed out each day, savoring the joy of being one day closer to freedom, reminding everyone at every opportunity how short I was. The banter went something like this:

"I'm so short, I can't step off the curb without a ladder."

"Oh, yeah? I'm so short, I have to reach up to tie my shoes."

"Ha! I'm so short, I can see eye-to-eye with an ant."

When I crossed off day 100, I became a "two-digit midget." When I crossed off day 20, I became "too short to see" and, in a Naval tradition that started well before my military days, I had a friend take my boots and hat and place them in line—work hat atop freshly polished boots—as a stand-in for me at roll call.

In the final weeks of my tour, I began giving away my uniforms, first the shiny "corfram" dress shoes that always pinched, then the extra hats—the squat, misshapen 1940's-era hats that all the women I served with despised—next went the thin raincoat that refused to keep me warm, and finally, my comfortable broken-in work jacket, all of which I wouldn't need anymore.

I kept my steel-toed boots and one work hat, which I still have. The Navy emblem on that hat—the eagle we called a crow because of its closer resemblance to that bird—is still tarnished green from the salt in the moist sea air. It was a symbol of my time at sea, a time when few women ever set foot aboard a Navy ship, much less sailed halfway around the world on one, that I wore like a badge of honor.

When I crossed off day number 10, my peers no longer referred to me as "short." With that stroke of the pen, I became "next." Being "next" meant that I was the next person on the ship due to be discharged. "Next" was what everyone on my ship who wasn't a "lifer" aspired to be. In honor of the joyous occasion, my friends and I threw a huge three-day beach party that became known as "Sharon's Short-timer Party." Everyone chipped in a little cash, and we rented trucks, tents and miscellaneous equipment from the Base Recreation Department and bought food and drink enough to supply, well, let's just say a whole lot of hard-partying sailors.

We pitched camp in a state park campground, the nylon tents mere yards from the surf. It was an idyllic setting and would have been meditative had there not been so much carousing. It was one of the most memorable times of my Navy career.

At one point, I convinced a group of sailors to pay me twenty-five cents apiece to ride up and down on one of the trucks' hydraulic lift gate. I would push the handle up and the gate would rise. Push the handle down and the lift dropped, lowering the sailor back to ground level. It was silly but fun. But the most fun was when I accidentally held the lever up too long. When the lift reached the top point of its travels it swung up at a 45-degree angle, and tossed the sailor into the back of the truck. It was a good thing he'd been drunk and relaxed at the time, or he might have been hurt. Believe it or not, he wanted to go again!

Two days after the party ended, I waved to my friends, heaved my duffle bag over my shoulder, and stepped off the gangway of the U.S.S. Jason for the last time. My heart thrummed inside me and my hands shook. Every part of my body sang with fear, excitement, joy, and sorrow. For four years I had been told what to do, how to dress, how to act. Now I would be on my own. It was like leaving home.

My stomach tightened as I walked, legs trembling, down to the pier and reclaimed my place as an ordinary "landlubber." Four years of my life had been given up to the military, four years in which I had traveled halfway around the world, followed orders, gained promotions, and been decorated. In four years, I had been assigned to four different duty stations in four different parts of the country, spent eleven months aboard a United States Naval Ship, and stood duty, as a bouncer in stateside enlisted clubs and as Shore Patrol in foreign ports. I had learned and laughed and loved and lost, but now that was all in the past. It was time to move on.

In the last few months of my tour of duty, I had considered re-enlisting numerous times, fear of the unknown causing me to doubt my initial decision to end my Naval service. As I crossed off the days on my short-timer's calendar, I worried about where I would go, what I would do. How much easier and more secure it would be to simply take the re-enlistment bonus and stay where I was. But each time, something inside me said, no. It was time for me to go, to do something else with my life.

The last time I rode the ship out of San Diego Harbor, headed for her new homeport in Hawaii, I participated in yet another Naval tradition. I threw my last 1940s dress hat over the side of the ship and watched as it floated, bobbing in the foam of the ship's wake along with several dress hats thrown by other sailors who would not make any more trips back this way aboard a Navy vessel.

After walking off the ship that last time, I took a cab to the airport and climbed aboard the plane that would take me back to the mainland. I was wearing civilian clothes and already, outwardly, there was no way for anyone to tell that I was, or had ever been, a United States sailor. I took a seat by the window and watched as we took off, rising into a perfect blue sky and passing through soft hazy layers of cloud.

As we leveled off, the realization hit me. I was free. I had served my country, fulfilled the longest contract of my young life, and now I was free to come and go as I pleased. But free to do what? I wondered as the fear came back, a dark furred animal rubbing up against the inside of my throat.

I hugged myself as I looked out the window. Before us, on the sky's horizon, was a rainbow. Every color glowed with light; each more separate and distinct than in any rainbow I had ever seen. It was flat from this perspective, not curved as it would have been from the ground, and we were flying directly into it—bright striated layers spreading across the sky before us—a vision I have not seen since. It showed me the promise of what could be, and the fear slid away, melting into joy. Again my heart thrummed and my body sang with excitement, but this time with no trace of fear.

In the moments of our lives when we sense the excitement of what can be, without the taste of fear, we are truly alive. In those moments we honestly give ourselves over to the wondrous birthing of new beginnings. How rare to have a physical symbol of that experience expressed as vividly as the prismatic display I flew toward on that final day of my Naval service.

D.C.

I had been to D.C. before,
but this time—
when I got off the plane—
it was so cold
the Washington monument had
shriveled to
one third its normal size.

I thought you'd be taller.

We go sightseeing and every entry
requires a new search,
security inspection of
bags and jackets,
emptying of pockets,
waving of electric wands to
magically protect us from
the terror of attack,
and I wonder
how much
plastic and duct tape it will take
to seal up my hotel room.

Souvenir vendors
sell tie-dyed patriotism made
in China and imported through
shark-infested waters.

And from the corner of my eye,
I see the figure of Abe Lincoln
leaving his granite seat to
kneel in prayer before
the black marble wall,
counting the names and
tracing the letters with his fingers as

his tears fill
the reflecting pool to
overflowing.

While across the Potomac
rows of headstones march in
long lines where
officers lie buried on higher ground.
The dates tell stories
and I notice that
while the enlisted almost always died young,
the higher the rank,
the longer the lifespan.

And the Women's memorial stands
gleaming in its newness
like an afterthought—
a remembrance built to
thank women for
their contributions to
freedom and liberty—
those of us
who served in uniform.

But I can't help thinking
this edifice stands
forgetful on the edge of
a cemetery filled with
thousands of children
mourned by
tearful mothers—

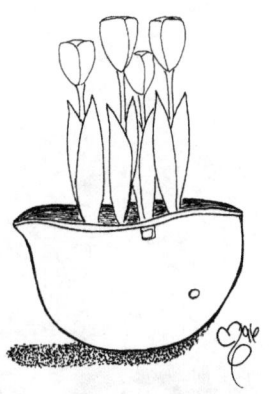

GUNS

While in the U.S. Navy, I served aboard a Repair Ship, the U.S.S. Jason. As one of the Petty Officers slated to stand the Junior Officer of the Deck watch, I had to qualify to carry a .45 caliber handgun. I was taken to the aft section of the ship, handed a loaded weapon, and told to fire directly off the tail of the ship. After emptying the pistol, I handed it back to the Gunner's Mate, who told me I had passed. Apparently, the distant waves were my intended target and, since I had presumably hit the water with every bullet, I was qualified.

you

I saw you, a bright light standing before me.
I, awash in the crowd. You, shining before us.

You shifted your weight as you bared your soul.
The rawness of it made me flinch a little.

The moment of your strength and certainty, powerful,
but passing just a little short of the time you needed to finish.

You deftly made your quick escape as if it would ease the pain
and discomfort from which your chosen words had flowed.

I love your beauty and your courage,
the way we've walked together hand-in-hand through fear,

And the way I see you,
as a bright light before me.

INHALING

On hot summer nights we stand in the front yard
        inhaling the smell of roses and lavender. The
world slows and stops sagging for a moment as
        we touch hands, kiss. In all my years I have never
been fond of people, but in you I have discovered
        there is an end to my cynicism. As we grow toward

one another, becoming more, the world treads softly
        near us. When life storms into the house, arrogantly
ignoring every "Do Not Disturb" sign, it is relegated to
        time-out, forced to sit in a corner considering the
inappropriateness of its actions. As time spins out
        my heart becomes the rose of peace, blooming

in my chest and casting out the deep shadows that were
        birthed there in my youth. I used to think that I was
born too late, that your early nature was beyond me.
        We come from different worlds, born into the same
time, moments that link like daisy chains strung by
        flightless fairies. When I discovered that our natures

could be so similar beneath all the differences, I shed
        my first true tears of joy. Salty, they were signs that
life existed below the cracked and barren plain I had
        painted as my heart. Misanthropic vines dropped leaf
and began to flower, and the beauty of the world peered
        in at me from behind clouds of smoke and crowded

streets. I still don't believe in fairy tales. Sleeping Beauty
        remains better off dead. But in small moments, I find
reality's harshness is a little less sharp-edged, a little less
        threatening, and I can almost believe in miracles.

people watching

We're sitting in the airport, waiting for a flight.
Face in. Better to watch the people. You point
out a "poser" on the payphone across from us.
Short-shorts, platform sandals, bright yellow halter.
She scratches herself as we watch. Her calves
are well-cut, but the rest of her is soft.

"She must bike," you say. I think she could be
an exotic dancer, high heels and bending over
causing the high-cut muscular look to her legs.
Her stance is obvious. She squats, knees splayed
wide, stands and bends over at the hips, the
movements of a trained provocateur, as women
with babies stream in and out of the restroom in an
unending cascade of motherhood.

People flow by in both directions.
No one looks happy as they go about the business
of travel. Some show weariness, wariness, and
even bewilderment. This is no place to be if
you have no sense of where you're headed.
Like life, you need to have a destination in
mind. But for some, there are no goals, only
the journey exists, one that will never end.

The Golden Garden

Here, my dear love brought to me
a table set beneath a tree.
A book, a pen, a sheaf of paper
pencils and tea. Amidst the landscape
I rested me, with pen in hand
and roamed the garden in my mind.
Sweet poetry, I blended there
with songs of birds upon the air,
and sweeter music could not be
heard throughout eternity.
My mortal soul hung meekly by
my weakened body, and as I
put my thoughts to page
I mused. They were as birds uncaged
the words that flowed out of my pen
and found their way to me again
in vibrance, as the lovely flowers
that o'erhung in leafy bowers.

AGAINST MYSELF

I lie curled inside myself—back turned against you,
Remembering the pain of not being touched,
Remembering the pain of being touched.
Wrapped within me, my warm heart,
Fresh with the blood of new thorns
Beats slowly, painfully, in agonizing thunder.
The tenderest place is the one I most fear to visit—
I keep recalling my defective memories,
Hoping they will be replaced with fresh thoughts
Spring-birthed.

If only I were able to cease the flow of blood, staunch it,
Reroute it around the vulnerable piece of me,
I would feel no pain.
Or joy.

The limitations of the frozen existence are what makes it most attractive,
desirable, and so expensive.

If I cry out in my sleep—put a pillow over my face,
It will block out the light and leave me in deeper silence.
Perhaps there I can sleep without these disturbing dream filled images
Of what it would be like to be loved—
To love.

When treading close to my heart, beware the forever fall
Into the deep abyss of self-denial and spiritual torture.
A black hole can only suck in life.
It gives nothing back, transporting all light to the other side of being,
Existence, a sunken apparition of what it used to be.

I always feared your touch—
It takes a special sickness to desire an empty, shallow husk,
To need to destroy the warm soul inside in order to touch the cadaverous
form of the undead.

Wrapping myself in the whirling chaos of confusion and denial
I could not gain access to the calm at the center.
The eye of my storm was blind and sterile and I was shut out
Into the cold battering wind.
Still it kept me sane—someplace where I could still reach myself,

Gently nudging and pushing toward awakening,
Away from that deathward march, and back into the warmth of
sunlight that danced over my pale cold skin like waves dance over the throbbing ocean
Spattering my soul with broken rainbow colors,
Pieces of the sanity I abandoned on the shore
at the edge of the infinite sea.

SOMETHING MORE

There were
never two younger children than we
were on our wedding day. But fiery
stones tumbled out of the sky and
doomed us to distrust and darkness.

There would
be future nights of conjugal bliss, but I
would not be a part of them.

The songs we sang were
pop culture and the dreams we wanted
had already been claimed.

Years later, you would
cry out in your sleep and tear at the bed sheets,
clawing to free yourself from the labyrinth. But
I left long before the ceiling began
to peel and the fireplace cracked.

Free from
circular bonds, I seek now to distinguish
wrong from not-quite-right, and to trace my way back,
following the breadcrumbs we left as we were led into
the woods, lambs prepared to slaughter
one another for the sake of something more.

Deadline

There are no shortcuts
As the countdown continues
And we are no closer than before

IN THE FIRE

Set me in the Fire,
to walk the smoldering coals of reality,
dance in the flames of
purification,
rise on cleansing Smoke.

Scatter my ashes to the Wind,
a prayer to reach the Sea.

Let me float into the Heavens,
where the Spirits of others
burn before me
and shine as the Light
of the Stars.

UNDRAWN SHADE

There is a window in my tombstone
A place for looking out and
Looking back.
A place from which to view eternity
from end   to end   to end.
No curtains dress the roughened edge,
No flowers grow upon the sill,
It looks the same on day and night.
No glass to clean the smudges from,
my soul sits here and gazes out.
From where I rest my heavy heart
I cannot see my home,
Or touch the hands of those I love
Nor gaze into their eyes.
The lack of joy descends on me
a heavy, heaving shroud.
As mourning breaks, a keening wail
that drifts away like smoke,
And staring out at what was lost
I find I am at peace.

FINAL RELEASE

I knew before they told me . . . You were dead.
The message on the answering machine didn't say.
It was just the standard, "Give me a call" sort of thing,
But I knew.
Knew that you'd finally gone and done it,
Given yourself an out, taken the path of least resistance.

Flesh can't resist the speeding bullet—
the lead pellets flying at lightening speed,
Through soft tissue, tender muscle, fragile nerves
and non-resilient brain cells,
Embedding themselves finally, in the wall,
taking with them tiny fragments of blood and bone
Where they permanently mixed with layers of paint
and old wallpaper.

And they said the stains wouldn't come out . . .
Out of the carpet, out of the couch,
out of the lives that you had touched.
The stains won't come out.
And now, the stains won't wash off my heart,
The crimson and violet stains that showed like bruises and
left black scars
Where you used to be.
Every place you touched you left your mark.
Your mark on the world is reflected in the blackened tissue
of the hearts that once held you in them.
The hearts that were open, until you closed them.
Closed them.
The way you closed the door and locked it one last time,
The way you closed the bullet in the chamber,
The way you closed your mouth around the barrel . . .
And your eyes, did you close your eyes?
Or did you stare at death with that cold blank stare that
you wore in your resolve?

Those times when you decided not to care anymore.

And I was startled when your spirit flew into my room.
I looked up at the sound. You hovered

suspended by your confusion,
Dazed, and a little surprised to find yourself there.
When suddenly, you needed to escape and crashed
headlong into the window.
Your pain and fear were all too familiar and
I knew it was you,
Recognized your hopeless, headlong flight into nowhere,
with oblivion dead on your heels.
You sat stunned, disbelieving the solidity
of the small glass panes before you
As I came to scoop you up and,
Once more, hold you before letting you go.

Your spirit fluttered a moment
Then sat utterly still in my hands as I told you gently,
that I knew you, felt you.
I said I would never hurt you intentionally.
You never believed it—till now.

And my last freeing act for us both was
When I carried you outside
And gave you
Your final release.

ON A GOOD DAY

On a good day, he walks to the mailbox to look for birthday cards and love letters, takes a walk in the park, buys flowers for her, and waltzes, holding her close until the moon sets and the sky blushes.

On a good day, he tells stories of heroic deeds, visits friends, wins at checkers three straight games, has time to read a good book, threads a hook with fresh bait and nearly snags "Old Grand Dad."

On a good day, he hugs his fourteenth grandchild, tucks her in, reads her a bedtime story, says a prayer for his oldest son who is traveling, helps with the dishes, and sits rocking on the porch late into the evening.

On a good day, he wakes early, makes fresh coffee, sits with her, savoring the freshness of a new day, making plans, discussing options, deciding what to do with their time now that they are retired.

She holds his hand, gazes at his thin face. Through her tears she traces the lines of tubing that intersect his body, keeping him connected, keeping him alive, and she thinks . . .

Today is not a good day.

YOUR PASSING

When we got out of the car and stood
   before the door (I still say the last building you enter
before boarding an airplane should not be called a
   terminal!) it was hot. Sweating travelers stood
on queue waiting to have their possessions
   tagged, lifted and sent on a separate path toward

the same destination, the way that you and I
   are now traveling. Flights came and went overhead
and for a moment I forgot to be sad. I stopped
   mourning your passing as I gave myself up to the
task of getting from point A to point B. The
   business of life continues without you, and I allow

myself to be swept up with the tide of it, though,
   in my heart, I am with you still. Holding you in the
final moments, watching as you close your eyes
   as if to sleep. I am tossed about on the tides of life
as you let yourself be swept out to sea, floating
   toward a light I have never seen except in dreams.

Your light will always be with me and, in the
   quiet moments between points, I will touch your
spirit and hold you once again, keeping you
   near me where we can both feel protected.

Another Grandmother Poem

I don't think she lost her mind.
She simply discarded it.
The Alzheimer's diagnosis was wrong.
She couldn't bear to remember anymore,
Swept up clouds of mist between herself and those she'd hurt,
Or those she'd been hurt by.

Her mind became an unused summer cottage where dust covers draped the furniture.
But selective memories become dangerous ground
And the dust covers spread and grew like evening shadows stretching into darkness.
Soon, only a corner or two stuck out,
in tiny moments of clarity.

"How did you find me?" she'd ask in surprise,
Not knowing herself where she was anymore,
And we would have to tell her again who we were.
She didn't know her own children had died
That all her friends were gone,
Couldn't recall having moved across country
Or all the years that had passed.
But she knew the natural color of my hair
And how many times I'd been married.
And I was no longer frightened of her—
Her weakness made me laugh until I cried.

My peace was made at the side of a deathbed
Where I could never kneel.
The healing comes with time.
And now, some nights I sit up trying to remember
Everything that I have ever done or said.
And I wonder if I will still know myself
After all my anger is gone.

My Mother Cyber-Dates

She is strong, able to appear emotionless,
Ready to move on, but my mother hurts.
Her heart crumbles even as she sits before the computer
sending email to a man she has never met.
She made a date with one last month,
called it a CO_2 date,
"no sparks," she says laughing into the phone.

In my youth, her strength seemed hard and
I never realized how deeply I cut her,
how much blood was shed from her heart,
a heart I thought was
puncture-proof.

Now, we share our painful moments,
commiserate over betrayals,
and thank one another for "being there."

The distance that once separated us
has become a geographical nuisance.
The once insurmountable differences,
a no-longer-hurdle we step over hand-in-hand,
like a cracked sidewalk we avoid in
superstitious reverence and fear.

And I, now a mother of step-children,
find that I have a hard strength to me,
a strength I use to cover up the pain of separation,
the distance I use as a shield
to allay the anxiety of departure and
the sadness of good-byes.

I have raised the banner of stern discipline
to slay the beast of closeness and
avoid reliving the feelings of an outsider

by remaining outside the sphere of emotion.

But when the cuts come, my heart will bleed.
My heart that has never been puncture-proof.

And I will call my mother, and we will share our pain,
commiserate over betrayals,
thank each other for "being there,"
and ultimately
laugh into the phone.

COTTON CANDY

My mother buys pink cotton candy
from a tall man down by the sea.
Sand between her toes,
she walks toward the pier
and dissolves.
Her face goes first
then her hands,
and the place where her heart should be . . .
The last to go
are her knees,
bruised from kneeling in prayer.
Prayer for the loss
of children's souls,
scorched by the sun,
turning to dust
and fine strands of sugar,
washed up on distant
beaches,
walked on by
invisible mothers.

ADA'S WISH

"Wishin' don't make a thing so. "Momma wiped her wet hands on the blue and white flowered apron she always wore.

Ada put her chin in her hands and squinted hard in Momma's direction. She wished with all her might, but nothing happened. Momma's hair still had the same streaks of gray and her eyes still held the same tired look they had since Sandy's death. It wasn't just the extra work of caring for the twins that seemed to have aged her though. It was something else.

Momma used to sing in the mornings when she'd come upstairs to rap on the door and wake Ada for chores. Ada would snuggle deeper under the thick, warm blankets and pull her pillow over her head. Momma would come into the room, yank open the curtains and say, "Rise up to greet the day, Ada Lynn. Them birds are singin' for you." Then she'd sweep the covers up with a whoosh that pulled in the cold morning air and let them float back down. Ada would roll out from under the blankets before they settled and skitter across the icy floor into the bathroom.

It was a game they'd always played. But now Momma just stuck her head in the door and said in a quiet voice, "Get up Ada, it's time." Nowadays, her eyes sagged and she moved like someone slogging through thick mud, and Ada didn't even think about staying in bed. She just got up and got ready for school.

Sometimes Ada thought that if she did everything just right, somehow, some way, it would change things and Momma would smile and sing again. But no matter how hard she tried, nothing seemed to help. A cold shadow clung to Momma and seeped through the whole house. Ada didn't even get scolded anymore. If she forgot to do one of her chores Momma only looked at her with her sagging face and said, "Ada, don't you have some work to do?" Then, without waiting for an answer, she'd turn and leave the room.

Ada wished her brother could still be here. Before he'd passed, Sandy was always doing something outlandish. Like the time he rode the old boar around the sty till it run under the lean-to and scraped Sandy off its back and right into the muck. Momma had laughed till tears slid down her cheeks.

The three months since Sandy's death seemed more like three life times. He'd never really been well after Kathleen had left him and the twins. Up and left without a word. Ada hadn't understood it. Still didn't. Why, even the meanest sow wouldn't leave her babies. But Kathleen had. One day, toward the end of summer, she'd gone and left the house and never come back. Ada remembered the way the pasture had turned that golden yellow color that glowed like fresh honeycomb and how everything had been warm and lazy. Even the bees were slow, their buzzing quiet, low whispers, like a church full of people on a Sunday morning waiting for the preacher to pronounce judgment on a host of newly committed sins.

Sandy drove up the dirt road so slow and deliberate that hardly any dust raised itself up off the ground. The old pickup truck inched along the road as Ada watched from the porch. Ada didn't even run out to meet him like she usually did. Something kept her stuck to the porch swing as the truck rolled on up to the house.

Momma came out wiping her hands on her apron. "Why, what a surprise! You're just in time for supper," she said, wearing her biggest smile. She stopped, the smile falling off her lips, when she saw that Sandy and the twins were by themselves.

Ada hadn't ever seen Sandy cry. He'd always been her big, strong, older brother, so tall and long-legged he could take the porch steps two at a time. He hadn't shed a tear in front of her, even when Papa passed on. But here he was, eyes red and swollen, leaning on the hood of his old truck with his brown hair uncombed, trying hard not to let go. Momma gathered up Jason and Eric, one pale, chubby body in each arm, and carried them into the house. "Ada, set the table," was all she said.

Sandy and the twins moved into the house that week. Sandy took the guest room downstairs and Momma put the boys in Sandy's old room where she could keep a close watch over them. Momma and Sandy never spoke about it when Ada was around, but she caught bits and pieces of what they said when they thought she couldn't hear. Momma said Kathleen was a bad apple, she'd always known she was a bad apple, but she couldn't hardly believe she'd stoop so low as to leave her own children. Sandy didn't answer back. He just sighed, like there was no more spit or fight in him.

That winter, Sandy caught the fever and Momma had to nurse him night and day. He'd seemed so much better at Christmas, and the house had felt almost warm. Momma cooked a great big turkey dinner with all the fixin's, just like she used to before Papa died.

But in January Sandy took sick again. "Too much, too soon," Momma fussed over him. Said he just needed to rest a while longer, but Ada knew it was more than that. His face held a sorrowful longing. His body sunk into the bed and he hardly seemed to know where he was. The sickness had gotten into his heart somehow and there wasn't anything that Momma or even the doctor could do. Not even the cries of the twins could rouse him.

They buried Sandy on a cold day when the wind soughed through the tree branches and cut though Ada's clothes and reached inside, numbing her to the core. Momma held the twins, her tears catching the light like tiny drops of frozen dew. No sound came from her, but Ada could see Momma's spirit twisting inside, like sheets tangled on the line in a high wind. The twins fussed in her arms, but Momma seemed unaware. She held them with stiff arms, like they were no more than a couple sacks of flour.

That's when Momma stopped singing. Now she went about the house doing everything stiff, like a wooden doll. Even when she was putting the twins to bed at night she was hushed and somber. No lullabies passed her lips. Just a low shushing and mumble of words.

Ada picked up her lunch pail and headed out the door. The school bus would be along soon. If Ada wasn't at the roadside stop, the driver wouldn't wait and she'd miss school. She tried to make herself pick up her feet, to walk with a purpose, like Papa had always said a hard workin' person should. But the ground pulled at her, slowing her down, her feet dragging against the dirt. She glanced back toward the house and saw two long streaks stretching out behind her in the dirt like fat snakes.

Why can't wishes come true? she wondered as she waited beside the narrow road for the school bus. *The teachers all keep saying what a powerful tool the mind is. That we only use a small portion of our brains. Who knows what amazing wonders a body could make happen if they put their entire mind to it? Why, I'd wish Papa and Sandy alive again and that old sack of catguts, Kathleen, in the ground instead.*

Ada kicked at a rock and sent it skittering across the road as a voice crept inside her head unbidden. Careful what you wish for, Ada girl. You might not like what you get.

"Now how can that be, if wishin' don't make a thing so?" Ada asked aloud. But there was no answer, just the holler of a magpie and the rustle of leaves overhead. "Leastways, I still wish Momma would smile again. Or maybe even sing."

* * *

It happened slowly. Ada had taken to spending time with the twins each day to give Momma a quiet spell from tending them. She'd offered to cook dinner too, but Momma told her she liked to cook. Though, Ada thought, you couldn't tell it by the way she shuffled about the kitchen like a thief trying not to rouse a sleeping victim. When Ada went into the kitchen and tried to help out, Momma would stop what she was doing and just stand there, staring at her till Ada put down the potatoes or the snap peas and left the room. Then she'd go about her slow-motion cooking again.

The twins were growing fast, shooting up like spring weeds. Eric, blue eyes glinting with mischief, was already walking on his own and Jason, only a little behind his brother, was able to stumble around the front room by clinging to the furniture with his stubby fingers. At first, Ada had walked behind them with a steadying hand in case they wobbled, but Momma scolded her. "Don't you pester them whilst they learn, Ada. They gotta learn to fall and pick themselves up."

"But what if they get hurt?" Ada asked.

"It's a part of growing." Momma closed her mouth into the thin, flat line that told Ada the conversation was done.

So Ada learned to watch and only interfered when one of the boys fell and bumped his head or got a scrape. Then she'd get a cold wet cloth to hold against the growing lump or sore spot, and rock the baby till he hushed his crying.

One Saturday morning, after chores, Ada took the boys out into the yard to play. Ada pretended to chase them, growling like a tiger and leaping at them. The boys giggled and tried to escape, run-stumbling on their short legs. The thick, green grass cushioned their chubby bottoms when they fell.

Then the boys chased her back, making noises in their throats and clinging to her legs. Soon the three of them were rolling in the grass, laughing. Eric got the hiccups and Ada chuckled at the surprise on his face. Then she heard a noise on the porch and looked up. There was Momma, one corner of her mouth turned up so slight, and gone so quick, Ada wasn't sure if she'd really seen it.

Then Momma turned and went back inside, the screen door squeaking shut behind her.

The next day, after church services, Ada heard a sound like a moan coming from the kitchen. She started toward the swinging door, but stopped as the moan turned into a low hum. Ada waited, listening. The sound came again and Ada smiled. Momma was singing! Well, not really singing, Ada thought, more like making sad music in her throat. But it was something. She stood in the hallway outside the kitchen, holding all the air inside her lungs. Waiting. Hoping. But the words of the song stayed inside Momma, still not ready to wing into the world.

From then on, Ada took special care to do all her chores and make sure the boys didn't have any reason to fuss. She even hung out the wash and brought it in again, folding and sorting the clothes just the way Momma liked. Each day, the cold seemed to fade just a little bit from around Momma's heart. "Not so's a body would notice if they weren't looking for it," Ada told the twins one afternoon as they gamboled about the yard, "but some."

That night, after dinner, Ada stood at the kitchen sink, staring at the soap bubbles. She swirled the water with her hand and watched the iridescent glow of the twirling foam. As the reflection on the bubbles turned from blue to green and violet, she found herself wishing again. Wishing that Kathleen had never left. Wishing Sandy were still alive. Wishing for Momma to sing again.

The pat-pat-pat of running feet and a tot-sized giggle trickled into her ears and drew her thoughts away from the spinning suds. What were the twins up to now? She snatched up a dishtowel and dried her hands on her way toward the sounds.

She paused in the hallway. Water splashed in the bathroom and a quavery voice trembled against the tiles and whispered out to where Ada stood mesmerized.

"He's got the tiny, little babies in his hands, " Momma's voice shivered, as if it had forgotten how to form the song and only now was remembering.

"He's got the tiny, little babies in his hands."
Momma's voice grew clearer, rippling into the hallway.

"He's got the tiny, little babies in his hands."
Ada's heart squeezed into a tight fist. The walls seemed to push in

on her.

"He's got the whole world in his hands."

Momma was singing again, singing for the twins. Ada covered her mouth with the dishtowel to muffle a sob and slunk back to the kitchen. She should be happy that Momma was coming back to herself. She should be happy that Momma could smile again, that she could sing. But she wasn't. She stood at the sink, scrubbing the towel across the salty streaks on her face.

How can she sing for them and not for me? She slammed the towel on the side-board. How can she? It was me, Momma. It was me. She seized the last dirty pot and scoured it, worrying at the metal surface till it gleamed against the yellowed sink. I'm the one who wished it. Her tears mixed with the soapy water. I'm the one you should sing to.

Momma's singing wafted out to the kitchen, accompanied by baby-boy gurgles and the splish-splash of bathwater.

Ada turned on the faucet, opening the tap as wide as it would go, to let the rushing water drown the sounds from the other room. Steam rose from the streaming water and beat against her face. Her eyes smarted as she stared at the seething cloud, refusing to blink.

This was all Sandy's fault.

Her hands clenched. If you'd never married that sow, Kathleen, in the first place the twins wouldn't need a momma. Wouldn't need *my* Momma.

Ada rinsed the pot, and set it in the rack to dry. Pulling the plug from the sink, she let the water drain out and watched the suds spin away, feeling small and empty, as if a part of her, the biggest part of her, had slipped down the drain with the soapy water.

"You were wrong, Momma," she muttered. "Wishin' can too make a thing so. Just not the way you want."

REGRETS

In the midst of regrets,
the world spins slowly,
adding its weight to the crush of blows.
In the beginning, there was need and fulfillment,
desire newly awakened.
As leaves faded and the garden, overgrown
with weeds, filled with rusted tools,
we paid homage to the greatness
of reality,
losing ourselves in the darkness
and letting go of the polished certainty of
black and white.

Where do we go now, my love?
You have ridden the skies of longing
until your shadow hung about you
like a winding sheet
and I have put aside my aspirations for the quiet
of an ordinary life.
How many fools will it take to recover our beliefs?
And when they reappear, will the ghosts of what
might have been relent?

I am haunted by a vision of old age and youth
forever joined in a hollow cavern.
I cry out in my sleep.
But you continue to dream . . .

and my heart remains an ancient prison
where dampness licks at the walls
and eats at the unguarded bars.

My tears are too close to the surface
of my soul and I cannot stop this spiral.

I dance into a wicked light where all I am
no longer matters, all I have been is a distant memory,
and all I could be lies stranded on a distant shore.

MEMORY

Forgetfulness comes too easily
And modern wisdom has no cure
For regret.

the cupboards match the floor

Posted on 2007.04.02 at 20:23

This past weekend, I removed the cupboard doors in the kitchen and pantry. Since the floodwaters destroyed the flooring, we figured we might as well paint before the new flooring gets installed.

This will be done in stages, as we still have jobs, and side jobs, and a nonprofit to run, oh, and teenagers.

As I said before, this is an old house and the people who lived here before us SUCKED at home maintenance. So, before I could remove the cupboard doors, I had to strip multiple layers of paint off the hinges to get at the screws.

One of the doors to one of the less used cupboards, high above the sink, was stuck. When I pulled it open, a portion of the wooden frame came away with the door.

So, now the cupboards match the floor, a lovely pattern in modern devastation. VERY chic!

NIGHT BIRDS

You wonder why your mother cries,
why your father's love lies
drowned at the bottom of a thick-sided
glass. She'll tell you that money
was never the issue. No, it was
bee stings and broken bones,
late nights and lost hours that left her shattered and
sad. Sitting with her back to you, she takes
another drag from her smoldering cigarette,
and exhales. Smoke curls up through yellowed fingers.
A cloud hangs overhead, and you wonder
if it is only smoke that wreathes itself about her,
stinging her eyes and bringing tears.

Your brothers and sisters never seem to notice
that when she cries the night birds stop
to listen, waiting for a cue. In someone
else's family, you might have been a saint,
a hero whose only weakness came from
a world far away. But here, you are the
one thing that cannot go untested. And you know
that you are the reason your mother cries.

There will be a time, one day, when
she will smile at you from behind flowers,
but the smile will fade as she drifts
into the distance, the white light of
hospital sheets reflected in the whites of her eyes.

For now, you watch as she wipes at her tears
with a calloused hand, drops ash upon the floor,
and lies to the neighbors, telling them that
children are clumsy, their lanky limbs
causing them to tumble and fall, that bruises
are all a part of growing up, and how
cigarette smoke irritates her eyes.

VEILED MOON

My darkness, Your light.
   My light, Your blood.
     My blood, Your vision
        floats by like smoke
from a brazier,
   swinging like a pendulum
and spilling ash upon the floor.

We were made before the sea
     washed in, before the towers fell,
        before the moon blanched and hid
           herself from the prying eyes of
ancient men in dark robes,

Worshippers and would-be gods,
     who wrapped themselves in mystery,
       stalking her,
  following her every move
in the name of power,
      Reaching for control of
        darkness
    under the guise of religion,

Warring against one another
   striving to be the first
      to steal her light
        and serve humanity,
. . . for a fee.

Looking back with cat's eyes
   the narrow way becomes
      the only passage, but
rebirth is premature.

We struggle against pain,
   fighting the universe's attempt

to abort being into
        nothingness.

Back against the wall
        I await the messenger,
  holding myself hostage before
the gates, searching for myself
        in your light,
                performing the ritual
passed from one generation to the next.

Riding the crest of spiritual spasms,
     lost souls become
        the cattle of a new age,
    Point-and-click people
  floating in the tails of trailing comets,
drinking toxic waste from false visionaries,
       and covering women's souls
  in the same
        dark veils once used to hide the
  beauty of the glowing moon.

She rises now, once more,
       a glowing visage of beauty,
  and symbol of who we are.
      Darkness and light
melded into one being.

My darkness, Your light.
  My light, Your blood.
    My blood, Your vision

      floats by like smoke
from a brazier,

  swinging like a pendulum

and spilling ash upon the floor.

SHADOWCASTER

I

Who is she,
this nameless shadowcaster,
who walks through my existence
cloaking the sun?

Opaque illusion
like a hand that passes
before my face.

Predatory vision in dark lines
and white spaces, devouring logic,
enabling my fears.

Residual offerings await her
with mock expressions
of faith.

Dark Mistress of my past.

Hostage-taker, dream-slayer.
Her promises still beckon,
smile at me,
taunting, tantalizing.

I would banish her from my private lands.
But she holds the deed to my desires,
mortgaged by lust
and just beyond grasping reach.

She grants no clarity of reason.
Lines twist in sanity's wake.
Rippling shockwaves expand outward,
heaving up toward blackness.

Ascension to the depths of my soul.

II

Instrument of death.
Mirthless music of finality
plays upon your strings.

Echoing discord.

Dance me through the gates as
the waiting processional wavers and flows
in spontaneous reaction to light and sound.

Arch of energy, reverberating,
coiling back to spring again.

Tempestuous tempo spills
out upon the freshly turned earth.

Play for me!

III

Silhouette that does not brush the earth,
shade of moisture and breath
dusting me with vital energy.
I have surrendered to your touch.

Editor of broken glass lies,
sub-zero relative to
your chilling inconsistencies.

I am the abyss.
Staring back at myself,
I become the prophecy
fulfilled.

The streets devour me
as homeless wanderers litter walks strewn with
glittering glass diamonds and
flakes of existence.

My mother
draws back the plunger to
fill me with the sugar-coated poison
of dysfunctional love.

I have been beaten down,
left alone to lick the wounds of a
victimless crime.

Happy memories bring tears of
pain and reminiscences of
bloody handprints
finger painting the walls inside my head.

IV

If this blackness could be emptier,
I would have something left to give.

V

Sssshhhhhhhhhhhhhhhhhhhh . . . .

Ebb and Flow

Ebb and flow—
The power of the dream
Spirits' greatest journey through
Visions sought and seen

Sojourn out of darkness
Guided by the light
To gain eternal wisdom
And the Shaman's inner sight

Abilities surrendered
Are given back in fold
To aid the seeker's final quest
Into the lands below

The river flows with knowledge
The circle is the key
The astral body sheds its skin
And finally . . . soars free.

MOONFLOWERS

They scattered moonflowers where she slept
And morning glories twined about the tree that gave her shade.
The grove where she had respite was green and lush and cool.
He knelt beside her daily
And spoke of all that he had seen in waking, dreams and visions.
He told her of the deeds he'd done and those still left to do.
He came to just be near her.
To feel her loving presence close was warming to his heart.
He felt he could not live without the brightness of her soul.
And when the days had caught him up,
Took from him the final draught of liquor from his cup,
They laid him down in that same place where he was wont to go.
So scatter moonflowers where they sleep
And let the morning glories twine about the tree that gives them shade.
Now side-by-side, through all of time, they sleep beneath the dew.

STATUESQUE

Gargoyles leering down at me from high rise perches,
Leaning precariously to give me
wet-dog, long-tongue, cement-hard kisses.
Walking freely through the cool dark courtyard,
neck stretched back, looking up,
Admiring
Pointed ears, stony staring eyes,
Strong hard claws closed tight upon cold stanchions.
Smiling in their dignity
Amassed about the rooftops,
I feel them
Safe-keeping me.

perchance...

With sleep as our guide
We are the guests of misted dreams
Upon the waves of REM.
Spectators to passionate lives
Exploding in chaos and disarray
To be reorganized into one act plays,
Soliloquies of angst, love, and yes, delight.
The fears that find us here are only haunting memories.
This is a private carnival funhouse
complete with twisted mirrors and oh-so cunning mazes,
Costumes and make-up to dazzle our eyes
and cleverly disguise who we see
As superheroes and villains.
The ultimate Virtual Reality—
And we, the key players,
Connecting one on one with the imagery of self
and selflessness
When
the buzzer sounds
and, finding ourselves unmasked,
We pose as unassuming mortals until . . .
We enter the phone booth of sleep
Once more.

Floating Leaves

I had this dream . . .

She was floating leaves in the house.

        It was surrealistic . . .

    They covered the floors and filled the rooms . . .
    Rustling across worn wooden floorboards
    that always creaked.
    Clinging to thread-bare carpets
    tread bare by years.
    Drifting through the once warm kitchen
    that still dreamed of fresh-baked bread.

She was floating leaves in the house.

        It was strangely artistic . . .

    Spreading them wantonly
    with the grace of her age.
    Her movements those of a painter.
    A performance artist
    Whose every movement is oblique,
    but meaningful.

She was floating leaves in the house.

        Her movements were mystic . . .

    Giving each room a singular motif.
    She'd sorted them by size,

Sorted them by color.
Some were shaped like lovers' hearts,
Others like jagged spears.

She was floating leaves in the house.

    It was surrealistic,
        And strangely artistic,
            Her movements were mystic . . .

    But,

        all I could see

            was the

                mess.

Time Curves

Time curves in on itself
and I lose the ability
to trace the lines of your face,
the slope of your back
as we lie close. Darkness
swells between us covering
our sins, hovering above
like a dying man's shade,
begging to be released.
Your breath
stirs the air about us as
a bird's wing, fluttering,
fluttering . . .
I slip behind the curtain
of drowse and memory
where dreams are mixed
with the sounds of traffic,
become
the songs of wild animals.
I slide through moments
strain against doors
locked by choices
made too long ago.
My reverie remains
unbroken until
it's time to put the cat out.

COLD NIGHT

Night,
Cold,
Clear.
Bare branches tapping against themselves
like dry bones in the wind.
Poe whispers in my ear
and in my pounding heart,
Of death and dying memories.
He knew the living dead,
Beyond cynicism,
Transcending pain,
Surcease found only in written artistry.
Giving formless ghostly hurts
Names and almost faces,
We disavow cathartic needs
To let our own wounds speak,
as if in sorrow finding morbid humor.
Perhaps some fears are put to rest
Where nightmares face the day.

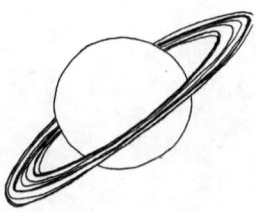

LOST ART

Luminous stanzas
form and fade
lost between
the last breaths of vanishing children and
dark moist dreams.

There is no Lizard King
and Sappho rests her pen,
ink drying in a cold
sea wind
that blows old heroes ashore,
drowned,

While white bulls and showers of golden mist
descend upon young virgins,
impregnating empty vessels
with heroic couplets and Spenserian stanzas
to be still-born on the wintry air of a snowy wood.

Form becomes formless,
rhyme ceases to exist,
alliteration waxes illiterate.

Pictures painted in dust on illusory landscapes
wither in darkness,
as words fail.

The Dancer

Oh, the music, the movement,
the drums and the bells

The swirl of her skirts
and the flow of her veils.

The bright woman dancing
who comes in my dreams

Is not who she looks like
and more than she seems.

The mother creator, the
daughter of Earth

Moonbeam and sunlight,
spirit of birth,

She dances and beckons
and leads me a chase

And I try as I follow, but
I can't see her face.

Now leaping and spinning
her movements a blur

She is charged and electric
with energy pure.

I reach for her hand,
her touch is unreal,

A tingling sensation is
all that I feel.

She gives me a message,
whispers it low

Then gracefully, slowly,
she turns and she goes.

A moment I stand there
in certain delight.

This time I will carry
her word into light.

But the image is fading,
awake in my bed,

Her presence a shadow
of mist in my head.

Night pulls off its covers
and shakes out the dawn.

The thought I'd held tightly,
but the message is gone.

Although I am certain
I'll see her again,

She comes when she chooses
I never know when.

Perhaps, if I'm ready,
the next time I'll see,

The message is mine for
The Dancer is me!

the vultures are circling . . .

I hear the voice of isolation screaming from your heart,
   as the tracks of reason follow you toward death
      with no one there to guide you.
Those who have gone before us left only breadcrumbs
      and the birds have feasted, leaving us to wander,
      lost in a valley filled with the soul of midnight.
The night touches us like a velvet painting,
      and my mouth fills with color as I try to create
      something of worth, something that will last,
      something that will fill this dark void with light.
The vultures are circling, and I'm not finished, yet.

www.ingramcontent.com/pod-product-compliance
Lightning Source LLC
LaVergne TN
LVHW051159080426
835508LV00021B/2701